122

THE STORY OF TH

JA

The
Story of the Irish Citizen Army

by

Sean O'Casey
(P. O Cathasaigh)

The Journeyman Press
London & West Nyack

First published, 1919
Reprinted by the Journeyman Press, 1980
with the kind permission of Oriole Editions, Inc

The Journeyman Press, 97 Ferme Park Road
Crouch End, London N8 9SA and
17 Old Mill Road
West Nyack, NY 10094, USA

ISBN 0 904526 50 X

The Journeyman *Chapbook* series

1. *The Ballad of Reading Gaol* by Oscar Wilde,
illustrated by Frans Masereel
2. *The Overcoat* by Nicolai Gogol, translated by
David Magarshack and decorated by John Edward Craig
3. *Shelley's Socialism* by Edward Aveling and Eleanor
Marx Aveling, and *Political Poems* by
Percy Bysshe Shelley
4. *The Radical Imagination: Frans Masereel*
by Josef Herman

Printed in Great Britain by
Interlink Longraph Limited, London

PREFACE

THE author ventures to hope that this humble attempt to reveal some of the hidden things correlative with the origin and development of the Irish Citizen Army will prove interesting to all who participated actually or sympathetically in the motives which inspired its creation, and, indeed, even to those who viewed its activities with suspicion and mistrust.

By many the budding Citizen Army, that struggled for expression and expansion in Dublin's streets, was a subject for amusing jokes and quiet laughter, and its actions were almost entirely ignored till the bud flowered redly on the second morning of Easter Week. Incidents are generally recorded as they occur, and few attempts are made critically to consider the circumstances that evolve them. The author hopes that the materials, carefully gathered together from original manuscripts in his possession, from notes recorded during the organising period of the Army, and from the contemplation of events in which the author participated, will be of use for incorporation in whatever history may be subsequently written around the events which culminated in the dramatic rising of Easter Week.

The author wishes, gratefully, to acknowledge the assistance he has received in the writing of the last chapter of this unpretentious work by Captains McCormack and McGowan, of the Irish Citizen Army.

It is impossible yet to say whether the events of Easter Week will achieve a Democratisation of Irish Nationalism, or whether the latter influence will deflect itself towards the broader issues of the Irish Labour movement.

Present events point to the probability that Jim Connolly's earlier ideals will be covered by the ever-rising tide of a militant Nationalism, though it also seems certain that the younger and more progressive elements of National thought will endeavour to associate with National advancement the upliftment of the Irish working class.

It appears certain that Nationalism has gained a great deal and lost a little by its union with Labour in the Insurrection of Easter Week, and that Labour has lost much and achieved something by its avowal of the National aspirations of the Irish Nation.

We can only hope that Nationalism, in its new-found strength, will not remain deaf to the claims of Irish Labour for a foremost place in the National Being, and that the sacrifices of Irish Labour through the Citizen Army may not be forgotten by those who are working towards the regeneration of our common country.

CONTENTS

THE STORY OF THE IRISH CITIZEN ARMY

CHAPTER I

THE FOUNDING OF THE CITIZEN ARMY

" The people were waitin' in thousands there,
An' you couldn't hear stir nor breath."
—*The Man from God Knows Where.*

DISCONTENT had lighted a blazing camp-fire in Dublin. The ruddy light of the flame was reflected by an earnest and ominous glow in the face of every Dublin worker. Men, full of the fire of battle, thronged in dense masses the wide, expansive area facing Liberty Hall. The city was surging with a passion full, daring, and fiercely expectant; a passion strange, enjoyable, which it had never felt before with such intensity and emotion. It was felt, unconsciously, that this struggle would be the Irish Armageddon between Capital and Labour. The workers were exuberantly confident that the unparalleled spread of the sympathetic strike would overthrow the moneyed hosts of Midiam. Did you not hear it? It was true, many great scholars had declared in their favour, and even now Captain White, the aristocrat and gentl man, was with their beloved Leader, and had signified his intention to throw in his lot with his socially humbler brothers, abandoning the privileges of position, ignoring the

remonstrances of friends, choosing freely and bravely
to stand by the people now in their hour of need.

And the eager, toil-worn, care-lined faces of the
workers now turned with concentrated uneasy patience
towards the window on the left-hand side of Liberty
Hall, waiting for it to be raised, that they might listen
to this nightly message of hope, progress and encouragement from those Leaders, whom they were convinced
would guide them safely through the heavy ordeal that
each man must share that there might be preserved to
all the elemental right of the workers to choose their
Union, and to follow the Leaders in whom alone they
placed their whole confidence and trust.

The disappearing Artist Sun had boldly brushed the
skies with bold hues of orange and crimson, and delicate
shades of yellow and green, bordered with dusky shadows
of darkening blue, which seemed to symbolise the glow
of determination, the delicate hues of hope, and the
bordering shades of restless anxiety that coloured the
hearts and thoughts of the waiting, watching masses
of men that stood silently beneath the oriental-coloured
panoply of the sky.

Suddenly the window is raised, and the tense, anxious
feelings of the men crowded together burst out into an
enthusiastic and full-throated cheer that shatters the
surrounding air, and sends up into the skies a screaming
flock of gulls that had been peacefully drifting along the
sombre surface of the River Liffey. Louder still swells
the resonant shout as Jim Larkin appears at the window,
with an animated flush of human pride on his strong and
rugged face, as he brushes back from his broad forehead
the waving tufts of dark hair that are here and there
silvered by the mellowing influence of Time and the
inexorable force of issuing energy from the human
structure. Again the cheers ring out, and Larkin quietly

waits till the effort to demonstrate their confidence and affection will give place to the lustful desire to hear what he has to say to them, while hidden under the heavy shadows of the towering Custom House a darker column of massive constables instinctively finger their belts, and silently caress the ever-ready club that swings jauntily over each man's broad, expansive hip.

Rumours had been circulated that Jim Larkin had forged a new weapon for the workers, some plan which, when developed, would make their resisting power irresistible, a power that would quickly change their disorganised, clumsy, incohesive units into a huge, immovable, unbreakable Roman phalanx.

Hope's ruddy flame was leaping in their hearts : this day would be an historic one in the unhappy annals of the Irish Labour Movement.

Perhaps this lovely autumn sunset would be followed by the dawn of their social emancipation.

And the lusty cheers died away to a droning echo, which was followed for a few moments by a silence that was so strangely sincere that the mass of people resembled the upright figures of an assembly in the shady and silent regions of the dead.

And then, with a sweeping gesture of his arm, that seemed to pass around that tremendous gathering and make them one with himself in thought and hope and action, Jim Larkin began to speak.

In rugged, passionate, vitalising phrases he told them " that they were engaged in the fight of their lives; that every conceivable combination had united its forces against the workers; that it would be a long and bitter fight between the Titans of Capital and the Titans of Labour.

" Therefore the workers must become disciplined organised, made of the one stuff in thought and action, so that in all that they would essay to do for themselves there would be a spontaneous unity of pressure and a hardened and impenetrable unity of resistance. The men must get to know each other. They must no longer be content to assemble in hopeless, haphazard crowds, in which a man does not know and cannot trust the man that stands next to him, but in all their future assemblies they must be so organised that there will be a special place for every man, and a particular duty for each man to do.

" They knew to their cost that a few determined men, determined because they were imbued with the force of discipline, led by men whom they looked upon as their leaders, could scatter, like spray before the wind, the largest gatherings of men, who, untaught and loosely strung together, would always be dominated by the possibility of fear and panic.

" If they would not agree to bring themselves under the influence of an ordered and systematic discipline, then they could never hope to resist the efforts that were being made to prevent them assembling peaceably to discuss affairs of their Union. By order and discipline only could they hope to secure for themselves the recognition of the sacred heritage bestowed by Nature upon every man born into the world—the right to live. All this must be changed, and he, with the help of Captain White, who would soon address them, was determined to begin the work now that would bring about this much-desired improvement in the strength and mutual combination of the various sections of the workers.

" Labour in its own defence must begin to train itself to act with disciplined courage and with organised and concentrated force. How could they accomplish this? By taking a leaf out of the book of Carson. If Carson had permission to train his braves of the North to fight against the aspirations of the Irish people, then it was legitimate and fair for Labour to organise in the same militant way to preserve their rights and to ensure that if they were attacked they would be able to give a very satisfactory account of themselves.

" They were going to give the members of their Union a military training. Captain White would speak to them now and tell them the plans he had to create from among the members of the Labour Unions a great Citizen Army. Captain White would take charge of the movement, and he trusted that the various Trades Unions would see to it that all their members joined this new army of the people, so that Labour might no longer be defenceless, but might be able to utilise that great physical power which it possessed to prevent their elemental rights from being taken from them, and to evolve such a system of unified action, self-control and ordered discipline that Labour in Ireland might march at the forefront of all movements for the betterment of the whole people of Ireland."

Like the loud rolling of a multitude of drums the cheers broke out again. This was what was long wanted —a Citizen Army! What could not Labour accomplish with an army trained and disciplined by officers who held the affection and confidence of the workers! Now they would get some of their own back; and vivid visions of " Red-coats and Black-coats flying before them " floated before the imaginative eyes of the Dublin workers filled with and almost intoxicated by the wine of enthusiasm.

And once again the cheers rang out as the tall, athletic figure of Captain White appeared, and his boyish face was aglow with gratification as he listened to the cheers that seemed to proclaim to him a ready realisation of the schemes he contemplated towards the disciplined consolidation of the lower orders in the battalionised ranks of an Irish Citizen Army.

Captain White told them that the work would commence immediately. He told them to attend the very next day at Croydon Park, Fairview, where they would be marshalled, divided into battalions, sub-divided into companies, and put through the elementary stages of military training. "This was a day of Hope for the workers," continued Captain White, "the definite result of their plans depended now on the efforts and sincerity of the workers themselves. The Irish Citizen Army would fight for Labour and for Ireland. He asked all those who intended to second their efforts by joining the army, and training themselves for the fight for Social liberty, to hold up their hands."

Almost every hand was silhouetted out against the darkening sky, and a last long deafening cheer proclaimed the birth of the Irish Citizen Army.

CHAPTER II

RENAISSANCE

" Everything indicates—the smallest does, and the
    largest does ;
  A necessary film envelops all, and envelops the Soul
    for a proper time."

—W. WHITMAN.

FOR some time the enthusiasm engendered at the great
meeting held in Beresford Place, " the old spot by the
river," flamed hotly in the hearts of the workers, tens
of thousands of whom were then on strike in Dublin.
Imposing drills were held in Croydon Park, the picturesque suburban headquarters of the Transport Union,
and thousands of working-men zealously endeavoured to
learn " the soldier's glorious trade." It was certainly
inspiring to watch the stalwart workers marching in
column of company formation from Croydon Park back
to Liberty Hall under the command of the indefatigable
Captain White. Everything looked promising ; the rank
and file were representative of every shade of thought
and every degree of national feeling. Here was the clerk,
the artisan, the labourer, the United Irish Leaguer,
Republican, Sinn Feiner and Gaelic student. These
were the fat days of the Irish Citizen Army, but, alas,
lean days were soon to follow. The people of Ireland
were not ripe enough to be shaken from the green tree
of Nationalism into the wide basket of an Irish Labour

Army. A Citizen Army can only be formed from a class-
conscious community of workers, and the Irish workers
still slumbered on in the dark shade of unawakened
thought. And the Irish Labour Leaders were forced to
devote all their attention and thoughts to the difficulties
which the mighty labour upheaval were hourly creating,
and they could not surrender to the Citizen Army that
regard which was essential if the movement was to
be made a permanent and ever-growing success. Nightly
meetings in Beresford Place; rallies in all the districts in
which the men had declared war on their employers;
midnight meetings in Liberty Hall, meant that energy
and force, which would have preserved the initial imposing proportions of the Citizen Army, were employed for
other purposes, more pressing, and calculated to overcome the terrible pressure that the employers were using
to crush forever the effort the exasperated workers were
making to assert the elemental liberties and rights of
their class. Entertainments were organised in the Dublin Theatres to provide food and clothing for the wives
and children of the locked-out workers; the food distribu-
tion entailed an enormous amount of organised attention;
the municipal elections, in which Labour endeavoured to
exert its influence on Civic affairs, exacted a further
contribution of time and energy, and all these activities,
which were urgent and necessary, robbed from the organisation of the Citizen Army that application and support
which alone would have made it the success that many
believed, from first appearances, it had already achieved.

But the principal events which most injured the progress and shook the stability of the Irish Citizen Army
at this time were the frequent arrests of the Labour
Leaders; the gradual and humiliating weakening of the
workers' resistance to the pressure of the employers; the
malignant penalising of the Irish Transport Union by

the hierarchy of commerce; and the establishment in the Rotunda Rink on the 25th October, 1914, of the Irish National Volunteers. Hundreds of men began to dribble back to work, and this meant that they had very little time to spend in the training that Captain White still carried on, in spite of all difficulties, in Croydon Park, in Liberty Hall, and in the Fianna Hall, Camden Street, which was placed at the disposal of the Citizen Army by the Countess Markievicz.

The penalty of dismissal which the united employers of Dublin held over the heads of the workers if they continued to remain members of the Transport Union caused, naturally, hundreds of men to abandon their connection with the Citizen Army, though comparatively few, happily, evinced the slavish weakness to respond to this threat by severing their connection with the Union itself.

The creation of the National Volunteers was one of the most effective blows which the Irish Citizen Army received. Thousands that had originally attached themselves to the Citizen Army passed over into the more attractive and better organised camp of the Volunteers.

Many, no doubt, preferred Caithlin Ni Houlihan in a respectable dress than a Caithlin in the garb of a working woman. Many also realised that the governing body of the Volunteers was eminently influential, and that the ban which was over the Citizen Army, like a dark cloud, because of its arterial connection with the Transport Union, was not to be chosen as a shelter, when they could radiantly enjoy the National halo that glittered around the whole structure of the National Volunteers. The old lingering tradition of the social inferiority of what were called the unskilled workers, prompted the socially superior tradesmen to shy at an organisation which was entirely officered by men whom they thought to be socially inferior to themselves.

And in spite of the fact that the most prominent members of the Executive of the Volunteers were those who had done all they could to snatch from the workers the right to join the Trades Union of their choice; in spite of the fact that many of those who controlled the local requirements or occupied a position on the local Executive had locked out their employés because they had ventured to assert the first principles of Trades Unionism.

It is difficult to understand why the workers chose to join an organisation which was largely controlled by their enemies rather than one which was guided and governed by the men who were their elected leaders in the social war against economic tyranny and oppression.

Looking back on this surprising anomaly, it becomes obvious that because of the undeveloped comprehension by the workers of the deeper meaning of the Labour movement, the call of the National Tribe appealed to them more strongly than the call of the Tribe of Labour. Years of National propaganda overcame the influence that had been exercised upon their minds by the fierce teachings of Jim Larkin and the quiet but equally effective reasoning of Jim Connolly. But the Volunteer movement enjoyed other less attractive, but equally real and tangible, advantages. They had, comparatively, unlimited funds with which to equip their members, while the money that Labour collected had to be devoted to the work of providing food for the workers, that these might live and not die.

The National movement, too, had, practically, the monopoly of all the available halls in Dublin and elsewhere in which systematic drilling could be carried on. An effort was made by the Citizen Army Council to induce the Volunteer movement to allow them the use of these rooms on a few nights each week, but the Volunteers were, evidently, determined to maintain their

advantage in this respect, for every request was answered
by a polite but very emphatic refusal to help the Citizen
Army to overcome this important and embarrassing
difficulty.

The leaders of the Volunteers were also in the enviable
position of being able to devote all their energies and
their whole time to the one work of organisation, an
advantage that told forcibly in favour of 'their efforts,
while the Labour leaders could only now and then snatch
a hasty moment or two in which to pay a little attention
to the fast vanishing companies of the Labour Army.

For some months Captain White worked gallantly,
trying to do the work of ten men, and making superhuman efforts to organise, drill and equip an army single-
handed, furnished with no help, and receiving very little
encouragement. But the inevitable happened; the drills
became irregular, the numbers continued to decrease,
and, finally, the Captain found himself reduced to the
command of one Company of faithful stalwarts, who, in
spite of all obstacles, had remained as a sure and trust-
worthy nucleus of the Irish Citizen Army.

Then Captain White began to lose hope. He seemed
to be building on foundations of sand. He had no outlet
for his energies. If Labour failed to rise to the opportunity that presented itself, what good purpose could it
serve for him to be eternally trying to accomplish the
impossible?

About this time the Labour organisation began to
retire to their trenches. The strike had waned, and,
finally ended, and Labour engaged again in the work of
re-organisation, making strenuous efforts to recover lost
ground and rehabilitate the forces that had been scattered
in the great social offensive of 1913.

It was then that the writer of this little work, in an
interview with Captain White, suggested that definite

steps should be taken to form the Citizen Army into a systematic unit of Labour; that a Constitution should be drafted and submitted for approval to a general meeting of workers; that a Council should be elected to see after the revival of systematic drills, to open a fund for equipment purposes, to arrange for public meetings, to form companies of the army wherever Labour was strongest, and to generally take steps to improve and strengthen the condition and widen the scope of the Irish Citizen Afmy. Captain White enthusiastically welcomed the suggestions, and promised that he would recommence the work with redoubled ardour if a strong committee could be got together to second his efforts. A preliminary meeting of sympathisers and members was then arranged for a following night, and Sean O Cathasaigh was deputed to make out an agenda and draft a Constitution, so that the meeting could decide definitely upon a determined and regular course of action.

The meeting was duly held in Liberty Hall, and amongst those present were :—Jim Connolly, Countess Markievicz, W. Partridge, P. T. Daly. Captain White presided, and Sean O Cathasaigh acted as secretary to the meeting. The proposed Constitution was the item principally discussed, and its formulas were generally approved of and tentatively accepted. On the motion of Jim Connolly, seconded by P. T. Daly, it was unanimously decided to hold a public meeting in the Concert Room, Liberty Hall, on March 22nd, 1914, to invite the workers of Dublin to attend, and to ask Jim Larkin to preside over the meeting, as it was felt by all that the Chief of the Labour movement should know all that was recommended before it was finally approved of.

The general meeting of Dublin workers assembled and filled the Concert Hall, and at 12.30 Jim Larkin com-

menced the proceedings. Before calling upon the secretary to the meeting to read the proposed Constitution,
he expressed the hope that all members of the Transport
Union would immediately become members of the Irish
Citizen Army. He told those present that steps would
be taken to provide a standard uniform for the army,
as this feature would tend towards keeping the men
together and infuse them with a sense of dignity that
would be lacking if they were dressed in the nondescript
garments of civilian life. A member would be sent to
England to secure accoutrements, and he asked those
present to co-operate in every possible way to make the
Army of Labour an effective and lasting success. Tents
would be procured, and during the summer months night
camps would be held in Croydon Park, which would be
a source of pleasure and healthful recreation for their
members. He counselled them to be careful as to whom
they would elect to the Council of the Citizen Army.
He was certain that attempts would be made to influence
or capture their organisation, or to wean it from its first
attachment to Labour Ideals, and, therefore, it was
necessary for them to take every precaution so that the
army might always continue to work for the principles
which it had originally adopted, and not be set aside
from its path by any outside or subsidiary considera-
tions.

He then called upon the secretary to read the proposed
Constitution, which would be considered and discussed,
clause by clause, each of which would be approved of,
amended or rejected as the meeting cared to decide.

The Secretary to the meeting explained that this
was the initial effort to lift the affairs of the army
from the unsatisfactory condition in which they at present were, and to begin work in a systematic manner to
consolidate and improve the conditions of the army so

that it might become an influential fighting force in the ranks of Labour.

The proposed Constitution was then read, discussed clause by clause, and unanimously accepted by the vote of the members present.

Its principles were as follows :—

1. That the first and last principle of the Irish Citizen Army is the avowal that the ownership of Ireland, moral and material, is vested of right in the people of Ireland.

2. That the Irish Citizen Army shall stand for the absolute unity of Irish nationhood, and shall support the rights and liberties of the democracies of all nations.

3. That one of its objects shall be to sink all differences of birth, property and creed under the common name of the Irish People.

4. That the Citizen Army shall be open to all who accept the principle of equal rights and opportunities for the Irish People.

Jim Larkin then asked one of the members present to propose the following clause for inclusion in the Army Constitution :—

" Before being enrolled, every applicant must, if eligible, be a member of his Trades Union, such Union to be recognised by the Irish Trades Union Congress."

This clause was then proposed by the Countess Markievicz, seconded by Thomas Healy, put to the meeting, and carried unanimously.

The election of a Provisional Committee, to hold office for six months, was then proceeded with, and the following were elected to positions on the first Army Council of the Irish Citizen Army :—

Chairman : CAPTAIN WHITE, D.S.O.

Vice-Chairmen : Jim Larkin, P. T. Daly, Councillor
W. Partridge, Thomas Foran, F. Sheehy-Skeffington.

Hon. Secretary : Sean O Cathasaigh.

Hon Treasurers : Richard Brannigan, Countess
Markievicz.

Committee : Thomas Healy, Michael Mullin, John
Bohan, T.C. ; P. Morgan, T. Burke, T. Blair,
C. Poole, J. MacGowan, T. Kennedy, P. O'Brien,
F. Moss, P. J. Fox, John Shelly, P. Coady, P.
Fogarty.

The following notes relative to the meeting appeared
in the following issue of the *Irish Worker* :—

" On Sunday, March 22nd, the first steps were taken
to fortify and extend the claims of the Irish Citizen
Army upon the Irish workers by the framing of a Constitution and the election of an Army Council.

" Steps will be taken immediately to form companies
and provide drill-halls.

" District meetings will be held to select officers and
elect suitable district committees. All Irish workers
should join the Citizen Army, which is prepared to
explain and define its Constitution upon any platform
in Ireland. Let the workers keep clear of Girondin
politicians, who will simply use the workers as the means
towards their own security and comfort. Let others who
may prate about ' the rights and liberties common to all
Irishmen.' We are out for the right to work and eat and
live. As John Mitchel says :—

" ' Let the canting, well-fed classes shout and rave as
they may. Where you see a respectable, fair-spoken lie
sitting in high places, feeding itself fat on human
sacrifices, down with it, strip it naked, and pitch it to
the devil.'

" We have a few of these things to pitch to the devil,
so we ask the workers everywhere in which these few

words are read to prepare for the advent of the Irish Citizen Army; to take the names of all who would be willing to join; to secure the advice and services of ex-army men, and to write for all particulars to the Honorary Secretary, Citizen Army Council, Liberty Hall, Dublin."

And so the Irish Citizen Army was changed from airy nothing, and made solid, and given a local habitation and a name, and it immediately began to forge its way into the stormy centre of Irish politics, giving no mercy and receiving none from those organisations whose operations were similar, but between which there was fixed, apparently, an impassable gulf of Ideal and Principle.

CHAPTER III

REORGANISATION

" What we believe in invites no one, promises nothing, sits in calmness and light, is positive and composed, knows no discouragement, waiting patiently, waiting its time."—W. WHITMAN.

THE reorganisation of the Citizen Army began immediately, and though zeal at times outran discretion, good and permanent work was done.

Two splendid companies of picked men were formed as the nucleus of the City Battalion. Captain White gave an order to Messrs. Arnott for fifty uniforms of dark green serge, and the men eagerly awaited their arrival. For the time being the rank and file wore on their left arms broad bands of Irish linen of a light blue colour, and the officers a band of crimson on the right arm.

In a short time a consignment of haversacks, belts and bayonets arrived, and for a few nights following there was a terrible scene of polishing, oiling and cleaning, in which work Jim Larkin showed an enthusiasm worthy of a young boy with a new toy.

The army was divided into units of half-companies; the Dublin Regiment was divided into three sections, the 1st City Battalion, the second North County Battalion, and the third South County Battalion.

Drills were held twice weekly in Croydon Park, which were conducted by Sergeant-Major Fogarty and Captain MacDowell, under the supervision of Captain White. These officers were ably assisted by Lieutenants C. Poole, Fitzpatrick and O'Byrne.

Finally the uniforms arrived, and then there was a scene that certainly rivalled some of the tragic episodes depicted in Dante's Inferno.

The Council decided that no man could be allowed to bring his uniform home till he had fully paid the cost, but the confusion of undressing and redressing whenever a parade took place finally convinced the Council that there was no other alternative possible but to permit the men to whom uniforms had been allocated to bring them home and to come to all assemblies and parades in full marching order to save time and ensure military punctuality.

The two first companies certainly looked picturesque and imposing in their dark green uniforms and broad slouched hats of the same hue, most of which were jauntily turned up at one side, the leaf being fastened to the side with the ever-popular badge of the Red Hand.

The Citizen Army made great progress in drilling during the summer months, for splendid facilities were provided for extensive manœuvring in the capacious grounds of Croydon Park, Fairview, then rented by the Irish Transport Union. But when the winter arrived, the accommodation in Liberty Hall was limited, and an effort was made to secure the use of the rooms used by the National Volunteers for a similar purpose. But it was evident that the Executive of this organisation were unwilling to give any encouragement to the Citizen Army. Several applications were completely ignored, and a written request to the Secretary of the House Committee of the Gaelic League premises, 25 Parnell Square, elicited

an answer in Gaedhilge, the translation of which was as
follows :—

" The House Committee,
" 25 Parnell Square, Dublin,
",April 12th, 1914.

" I received your letter concerning our hall last night.
It is engaged now every night, except Saturday, and on
this night it is occasionally wanted for a social.   The
Volunteers use the hall on Tuesday and Sunday nights,
and *I don't think* the Committee would give it to *any
other organisation* for drill.

"The caretaker has now a good deal of work to do, and
the women, also, who are engaged to keep the hall clean.
However, I will put your letter before my Committee at
their next meeting, which will not be held till the begin-
ning of next month.—Yours,

" G. IRVINE, Secretary."

In fact, it was plain that, as far as encouragement and
support were concerned, the workers would have to rely
upon themselves, but it is certain that the lack of suitable
places in which to carry on systematic drill materially
interfered with the progress and growth of the Citizen
Army.

A manifesto to be sent to the various trades bodies in
Ireland was drafted, and, having been submitted to the
Army Council, and approved of by them, it was despatched to labour organisations in Cork, Belfast, Derry,
Sligo, Limerick, Kilkenny, Waterford, Dundalk, Galway
and Wexford.   This manifesto declared the principles
that the Citizen Army stood for, and asked the secretaries
of the Trades Union to make preparations for public
meetings in their several districts, which would be addressed by the Labour Leaders when an opportunity presented itself.   The manifesto pointed out that all political

organisations were preparing for serious eventualities; the Ulster Volunteers in the North; the National Volunteers were establishing companies everywhere in Ireland, while the lazy Hercules of Labour was content to lean on his club, indifferent to the stirring of all around him. " Would it not be a shame," declared the manifesto, " if the forces of Labour alone were content to believe all things; endure all things; to starve rather than to take; to be stricken and not to strike back ?"

The manifesto was partially successful in arousing an interest in the work and objects of the Citizen Army. Efforts were made to respond to the appeal in various places, but, on the whole, the battle went with the strong, and the National Volunteers effectively held their advantages almost everywhere, outside of those places in which the Irish Transport Union still carried on the fight for human emancipation.

The first definite meetings held to establish a company of the Irish Citizen Army, outside of Dublin, were held in Lucan and Clondalkin, on Sunday, April 12th, 1914. Announcements had been made that meetings would be held in these districts, and early on the Sunday morning the Countess Markievicz, Captain White, P. T. Daly, and Sean O Cathasaigh proceeded to Lucan in the Captain's motor-car to commence the shaping of the definite destinies of the Irish Citizen Army.

It was a happy spring day, and everything in nature seemed to laugh quietly at the querulous efforts of man to solve the complex human problems with which he was surrounded. We had no thoughts to spare on the loveliness that peeped at us out of every corner as the car swung towards Lucan, and our eyes were closed to the bursting buds, and our ears stopped to the singing of the birds, for in our hearts were commingling thoughts that painted pictures of the hope of success and the fear of defeat.

When we reached Lucan things looked far from promising, for we were silently and curiously received by a few stragglers, that stood here and there about the village, and seemed to be in no way desirous of helping in the promotion of anything that Labour stood for. After a very pleasant tea in a local restaurant, the Captain motored to a suitable place in the vicinity of the village, and, standing on the car seat, waited a few moments, while a shy and obviously timorous crowd of about five hundred people slowly gathered around the car, and displayed a demeanour of such ominous quietude that plainly revealed to us that the Irish Citizen Army had a long and energy exhausting struggle in front of it before the rural workers would become sufficiently class-conscious to understand the elementary principles of Labour thought and aspirations.

Captain White opened the meeting, and told them that necessity itself should force them to make an effort to safeguard their interests. P. T. Daly and the secretary followed, but much more interest was evinced in the passionate and nervous eloquence of the Countess Markievicz. During the progress of the meeting twenty names were taken by the secretary, and these were authorised to hold a subsequent meeting to elect officers and arrange for drills, and, in the centre of a rousing and sincere cheer, the motor-car sped out of the village of Lucan on its way to the more distant village of Clondalkin. The residents in and around Clondalkin evinced the same diffidence in coming together, and stood afar off for quite a long time, gazing fixedly towards the Captain's motor-car as if it were some dangerous machine calculated, if approached too closely, to upset for ever the quiet rhythm of the pastoral life of Clondalkin's inhabitants.

After some hours of waiting our patience was rewarded, and a fairly successful meeting was held, over which Michael Costello, the Transport Union delegate for the district, presided, and after its conclusion the car was turned head homewards, and we arrived shortly afterwards at Liberty Hall, by no means satisfied at what we had achieved, but fully conscious that we had bravely faced enormous difficulties and thoroughly convinced that the work of building up the Irish Citizen Army would be a long, arduous and painful task.

On Sunday, April the 19th, 1914, meetings were held in Coolock and Kinsealy, at which Jim Larkin, Daly and O Cathasaigh spoke, and in Swords, on the same day, a further meeting was addressed by these speakers, ably seconded by Captain White, who had proceeded to Swords after a parade in Croydon Park. A poster had been previously issued which called upon the " Men of Fingal! to join the Irish Citizen Army, that stands to defend the fair and just claims of the workers for opportunities to live honest, upright and cleanly lives."

On Friday, April the 24th, an enthusiastic meeting was held in Finglas, over which Frank Moss presided, and the speakers were, M. O Maolain, J. Magowan and S. O Cathasaigh. So in spite of many difficulties the Irish Citizen Army was making steady progress, and companies now had been formed and were actively drilling in Clondalkin, Lucan, Swords, Finglas, Coolock, Kinsealy and Baldoyle. The Irish Citizen Army had been officially recognised and approved of by the Trades Council on the 6th of April, 1914, and the delegates present gave a very warm welcome to the earnest appeal for their support and co-operation made by the Countess Markievicz and Richard Brannigan on behalf of the objects and aims of the Citizen Army.

Difficulty followed difficulty, but still the Army Council

refused to realise that anything could permanently with-
stand the onward march of the army. The Council had
to fight the vindictive hostility of the puffed-up employers, who had succeeded in plucking many useful
feathers from the growing wing of Labour; they had to
regard the silent but relentless antipathy of the officials
of the National Volunteers; they had to consider the
shattered courage of the Dublin workers that created a
condition of secret determination never to be openly
identified with Liberty Hall; and, last of all, they had to
passively submit to the irritating indifference of the
Transport Union officials to the .work that needed the
help of every available man. P. T. Daly spoke at many
meetings, but, with the one exception of Councillor
Partridge, no other official of the Transport Union or of
the Labour movement in Dublin, stirred a hand in the
development of an organisation which they all sincerely,
we feel sure, hoped to see the pioneer guard of the militant
Irish Labour movement.

Many a time members were prompted by the feelings
of hopeless endeavour to take their hands away from a
heavy plough that seemed to be ever ploughing the
sand.

CHAPTER IV

THE QUARREL WITH THE NATIONAL VOLUNTEERS.

" *Plantagenet* : The truth appears so naked on my side
        That any purblind eye may find it out.
Somerset : And on my side it is so well apparell'd,
        So clear, so shining and so evident
        That it will glimmer through a blind
        man's eye.".

—*Shakespeare*.

A SHARP, definite and lasting antagonism was born during the night on which the National Volunteers were established between the official controlling power of that body and the Labour movement in general.

Some of the most prominent speakers at the initial meeting, held in the Rotunda Rink, Dublin, on Tuesday, November the 25th, had been, and indeed were then, intimately associated with the effort to smash the Labour movement, and violent opposition was manifested by a large section of the audience towards these as they were advocating the reasons for Irishmen to unite in the Volunteers for the maintenance of the " Liberties and Rights common to all Irishmen."

It was generally concluded at the time that this disturbance was deliberately organised by the Irish Citizen Army, but the facts are that the army or its officials had nothing whatever to do with the occurrence, nor did any of its officers ever suggest that such an action would meet with their tacit consent or definite approval.

Efforts were made frequently by Captain White and by the Secretary to promote co-operation in the use of halls for drilling purposes, but no concession whatever in this respect would be granted by the Volunteers to the Citizen Army. Their original manifesto had been signed by members of the Hibernian organisation and by a member of the United Irish League, two movements that were bitterly and implacably opposed to the interests of Labour. Every political movement had received an invitation to attend the preliminary meeting, while Labour was silently ignored. In *Irish Freedom* every political body was welcomed into the National Volunteers, but no mention was made of the workers' organisations.

At a meeting held in Navan Mr. John MacNeill had announced that the National Volunteers would be under the control of the Irish Parliament, which Mr. Redmond had declared would be subservient to the English Imperial Parliament, and these incidents and declarations filled the mind of Irish Labour with so much mistrust and suspicion that definite and organised hostility began to be displayed by the Irish Citizen Army towards the efforts of the National Volunteers to induce the Irish workers to join its ranks. A vigorous discussion was carried on in the *Worker* by Seumas Mac Gabhan, a well-known Sligo Volunteer, and the Secretary of the Citizen Army. An effort was made by the Volunteers to form a company in Swords, a stronghold of the Irish Transport Union, but the meeting, which was kept secret till the last moment, was attended by officers of the Irish Citizen Army, who proceeded to Swords by car, and a strong company of the latter organisation was formed from those workers who had gathered together to hear the speakers sent to Swords by the Executive of the National Volunteers.

The Volunteers were asked if John MacNeill's statement was true; to declare if they stood for Home Rule, the principles of Grattan's Parliament, or an Irish Republic; to give in their Constitution a declaration in favour of the Rights of Man as well as the Rights of Ireland, as the United Irishmen did; and to refuse a welcome to those who attempted to prevent the workers from asserting their elemental right to join the Union of their choice.

At the suggestion of Jim Larkin, the Secretary of the Citizen Army sent to the Secretary of the Irish National Volunteers the following challenge :—

" To the Provisional Executive of the Irish National Volunteers :—

" Whereas, the Provisional Executive of the Irish National Volunteers have claimed from public platforms and in the Press the support of the Irish workers; and, whereas, the rank and file of the movement are almost wholly composed of members of the working class; and

" Whereas, the conviction is growing stronger in Labour circles, owing to the ambiguous principles of the Volunteers' Constitution, and the class basis of the Provisional Executive, and the Ladies' Auxiliary Committee, and the strong elements co-operating with the movement, which have been consistently antagonistic to the lawful claims of Labour :

" We the members of the Council of the Irish Citizen Army, representative of Organised Labour, now challenge the Executive of the Irish National Volunteers to public debate in which to justify their appeal for the sympathy and support of the Irish working class.

" Details of debate to be arranged by three members of

the Volunteers' Executive and three members of the
Council of the Irish Citizen Army.

> " (Signed) SEAN O CATHASAIGH,
> " Hon. Sec., Irish Citizen Army."

The following reply, written in Irish, was received
from Mr. John MacNeill :—

> " 19 Herbert Park, Dublin.

" DEAR SIR,—I received your letter last night at the
Volunteers' Headquarters, and I gather from its contents
that you think that there is a distinction being made by
the Volunteer Executive between the noble and the
obscure, the rich and the poor, and that you wish to
discuss the matter in public debate.

" I am ignorant of the existence of such a distinction.
I never heard much or little of it till I read your letter.
It is impossible for me to enter into a discussion upon a
matter about which I know nothing.

> " Sincerely yours,
> " EOIN MACNEILL.

" The Secretary, Irish Citizen Army."

This letter was succeeded by a reply subsequently
received from Mr. Gogan, Assistant Secretary to the
Irish National Volunteers, which ran as follows :—

> " The Irish Volunteers,
> " 206 Great Brunswick Street,
> " Dublin, May, 1914.

" DEAR SIR,—With reference to your challenge to
public debate, the Provisional Committee regret to say
that they cannot see their way to participate.

> " Fraternally yours,
> " THE HON. SECRETARIES.
> " (Per L. G. Gogan, Assist. Sec.)

" The Secretary, Irish Citizen Army "

The following comment on these letters appeared in an issue of the *Irish Worker* dated June 13th, 1914 :—

" We venture to draw the attention of the readers of the *Worker* to the fact that the challenge was first answered by Mr. MacNeill himself without consulting his Executive—a singular action—and also that the subsequent letter from the Assistant Secretary includes the rejection of the suggestion of a conference between three members of each committee to discuss the whole question. Is it any wonder that Labour looks dubiously upon a movement which is afraid or unwilling to give an answer for the hope that is in it? These replies are eloquent testimonies to the workers that the National Volunteers' attachment to Democracy is built upon foundations of hay and straw and stubble."

It is singular to relate that notwithstanding the acute feelings of antipathy that existed between the official elements in the Volunteers and Labour, the cordial relations between the rank and file of both organisations remained warm and apparent. It was a pleasure, when the Citizen Army accidentally encountered a body of Volunteers on the march, to see how eager both were to do honour to each other in an earnest and brotherly salute.

It was also strange that the Labour Leaders were always enthusiastically received everywhere, though their speeches were usually punctuated with sharp and penetrating criticisms of the Volunteer movement.

At a meeting held in Bray, on April the 15th, 1914, outside of the Town Hall, which had been let to the Volunteers to hold an organising meeting, but which was refused to the Citizen Army, though its use had been sought for the same purpose, the greater part of the audience consisted of members of the Volunteer movement. Yet Jim Larkin and Captain White got a rousing reception, and Larkin's impassioned appeal to all to follow the principles of Wolfe Tone and John Mitchel, in spite of the back-boneless Volunteer Executive, was received with a loud and an earnest cheer. Jim advised all the workers to identify themselves with the Citizen Army, and reminded them that to suffer for Ireland and for humanity was to enter into a brighter and a fuller heritage.

The antagonism of the official element in the National Volunteers was painfully demonstrated by the following announcement which appeared in the *Irish Worker* from the Labour Day Committee, May, 1914 :—

" Judging by the number of delegates present at last meeting, the celebration of Labour Day this year promises to eclipse anything held in recent years, notwithstanding the fact that the National Volunteers have organised an opposition demonstration for the same day."

One day while the Secretary was preparing an agenda for a Council meeting, a messenger arrived who told him Captain White was very eager to speak with him on the telephone. The Secretary answered the call and was astonished to hear Captain White say that he had received an astonishing letter from Mr. MacNeill; he went on to tell the Secretary to summon a Council meeting at once, " for," said he, " the Lord has delivered John MacNeill into our hands." It was explained at the Council meeting held that night that Captain White offered the Volunteer Executive two companies of fully uniformed and equipped men, if the Executive would allow them to remain an independent though affiliated body. This offer, with which the Citizen Army Council had nothing to do, and about which they knew nothing at the time, was made subsequent to the celebrated encounter which Captain White had with the

police while leading a few hungry men to the Mansion
House with a view of protesting against the organised
attempt to intensify unemployment in Dublin, that the
men might continue to suffer for their temerity in resisting the tyranny of the employers. The letter which was
sent by Mr. MacNeill, and which was read to the Council, rejected the Captain's offer, and explained that the
National Volunteers could have no association with an
organisation that had recently been in conflict with the
police. Several members urged that this letter should
be immediately published, but it was finally decided that,
as the Citizen Army had no intention of amalgamating
with the Volunteers, the wiser course to adopt was to
pass the incident over.

Looking over past events now in the calm of new
thought, it is painful to reflect upon a division that perhaps could not have been avoided but might indeed have
been less bitter. The men in the National movement
who understood and sympathised with Labour might have
been more tolerant, and probably would have been so,
had those in the Labour movement who understood
National Ideals been more forbearing.

During the whole controversy Captain White and
Countess Markievicz separated themselves from and frequently opposed the antagonism displayed towards the
National Volunteers. And it is most probable had any
indication been given by the Executive of the Irish
National Volunteers to promote an amicable understanding between two bodies who had so much natural affinity
with each other, that the influence of these two Leaders
of the Citizen Army Council would have evolved a working basis of genuine and useful unity between the two
organisations, with results that would have materially
benefited and strengthened the objects for which both
were ostensibly and actually working.

But there was one man whose voice was seldom heard, whose personality was little known in the Labour movement, but who was almost worshipped in the National camp, that silently but effectually opposed any corporate union between militant Nationalism and Labour. It was only when the star of this genius began to fade, which happened after his attempt to hand over the National Volunteers to the guidance of the Parliamentary Party, that a definite spirit of evident comradeship began to manifest itself between the Volunteers and the Irish Citizen Army. This man's persistent attitude towards Labour was the attitude of the witches towards the intrusion of Faust and Mephistopheles :—

" Who are ye? What would ye here? Who hath come slinking in? The plague of fire into your bones !"

This man was Bulmer Hobson, whose warmest appreciation of all things appertaining to Labour was a sneer, and whose influence, which was powerful and potent, even with those whose sympathies were undoubtedly with the working-class, was always directed towards the prevention of an understanding between the forces of Labour and the militant power of young-hearted Nationalism.

But during all this unfortunate strife the Citizen Army was painfully developing its strength, adding to its members slowly, but surely, till, at a meeting of the Army Council, it was at last announced that the roll-book showed that the Citizen Army in the City and County of Dublin numbered a thousand men.

CHAPTER V

PILGRIMAGE TO BODENSTOWN, 1914

" Oh ! sweet 'tis to think that such faith can remain
To the Cause and the Man so long vanquished and
slain."

—DAVIS.

ON June, the 26th, 1914, a pilgrimage was made to
Bodenstown under the auspices of the Wolfe Tone
Memorial Committee, and the Citizen Army Council
decided to participate. Vigorous preparations were
accordingly made for a full muster of members, for we
all knew that Jim Larkin had expressed his determination
to visit the grave of Theobald Wolfe Tone. The Secretary visited the Wolfe Tone Committee to procure
tickets ; and though some of the Wolfe Tone' Executive
doubted the wisdom of encouraging the Citizen Army
to participate, because of the differences between them
and the Volunteers, who were to attend in full strength,
the Chairman, Mr. T. Clarke, warmly welcomed the
suggestion, and personally undertook to be responsible
to the Wolfe Tone Executive for the good and earnest
intentions of the Irish Citizen Army.

On the Saturday previous to the day on which the pilgrimage was to be held, the President of No. 1 Branch
of the Transport Union came to the room where the
members of the army were assembled, and appealed to
them to abandon the enterprise, as it was essential that

every available man should be present at the general
meeting which was to be held the following day in Croydon Park to consider the resignation of Jim Larkin from
the position of General Secretary to the Transport
Union.

A messenger was hastily despatched to discover if
Jim was determined to carry out his intention of accom-
panying the pilgrimage to Bodenstown, and upon an
answer in the affirmative being brought back by the
messenger, upwards of two hundred men declared that
they would accompany their chief. The first and second
companies, headed by the Fintan Lalor Pipers' band,
marched from Liberty Hall to Kingsbridge, and were
met there by Jim and his eldest son, Seumas. The
members were at first somewhat diffident as to the reception that would be extended to them, but their doubts
in this respect were shortly set at rest by the kind and
cordial welcome given to them by Tom Clarke, who
appointed a special orderly to look after the Citizen
Army, secure particular carriages for the members, and
provide a special apartment for Jim and the members of
the Army Council. The march to Bodenstown was a
memorable one ; large crowds lined the narrow streets of
Sallins, and Jim Larkin, " the great Labour Leader,"
was the observed of all. The march past, in a field contiguous to Bodenstown graveyard, was an impressive
spectacle, and certainly, without expressing any undue
partiality, the members of the Irish Citizen Army, in
appearance and in technical movements, left little to be
desired.

At a subsequent meeting, held around the grave, it
was gratifying to see that the committee in charge made
every possible effort to give equal honour to all. The
Fianna formed an inner ring around the grave, and the

outer ring was formed by alternate members of the Volunteers and units of the Irish Citizen Army.

On the return journey a desperate attempt was made in Sallins by a great crowd of villagers who had assembled together to induce Jim to deliver a speech, but this he refused to do, because, as he said, he was the guest of the Wolfe Tone Memorial Committee, and all arrangements were in their hands, and he could not possibly allow himself to interfere with the arrangements that had probably been made weeks before the date fixed for the Pilgrimage.

It was a journey never to be forgotten, for it heralded the possibility of a closer unity and a fuller understanding between the Irish Citizen Army and the National Volunteers.

It was the first time they had stood side by side, the first time they had received and taken orders from a common commander, and this drawing together was possibly a symbol of a union that would be finally cemented together with the blood of both organisations.

From the issue of the *Irish Worker* succeeding the Pilgrimage, the following extract from an article that appeared in that journal is taken :—

" At the meeting, held in a field contiguous to the graveyard of Bodenstown, we were advised to regard the points of agreement between different sections of Irishmen rather than the points of difference between them.

" We venture to suggest that the Republicans should act upon their own counsel and take into consideration the points of agreement between themselves and the workers' organisations. If they took time to consider this over, they would discover that all workers are, through the force of necessity, potential rebels. Wolfe Tone held no foolish hopes of the union of all classes. He hated the aristocracy and thoroughly despised the propertied class and the merchants. He saw that these served only their own interests, and looked with affection, not upon Ireland, but on the stake they had in the country and the business they carried on in Ireland. He passed by the members of the Ascendancy Church, and linked up the oppressed Catholics with the equally oppressed Presbyterians. This union created the Society of United Irishmen.

" To-day the only possible union that Republicans can hope for is a union between themselves and the workers, whose principles are practically identical with their own."

It seemed that the fraternal association of Citizen Army soldiers and Volunteers around the grave at Bodenstown had started in the breasts of both organisations a desire for closer communion in thought, principle and action.

CHAPTER VI

THE SOCIAL SIDE OF THE ARMY

" Wi' merry songs and friendly cracks,
   I wat they did na weary;
An' unco' tales an' funny jokes,
   Their sports were cheap an' cheery."

                                        —*Burns.*

THE daily and nightly routine of the Citizen Army was sensibly relieved by many merry events which lightened the dull gloom of monotonous organisation. In a great marquee which had been erected in Croydon Park during the summer months, every Sunday evening, popular concerts were held, at which the members of the army, their sweethearts, friends and relatives held high revel. Dancing, singing and piping kept the night perpetually young, and, after a hard week's work of drilling, parading, and routine duties, these gatherings were a welcome change, when discipline was relaxed, and the officers remembered they were human and joined hilariously in the fun and frolic of the moment.

Jim Larkin was the life and soul of these gatherings, and frequently the audience would imperiously demand " a song from Jim," who, after some coaxing, would, like the shy boy he sometimes was, sing in a hoarse, tremulous voice, amid a tense and reverent silence, the " Red Flag " or " The Risin' o' the Moon." And the deafening applause, that would make the stained flaps of the marquee shake with terror after the song had terminated, would have gladdened the heart of even Caruso.

During this time Jim Connolly was busy writing Labour Songs, and " Freedom's Pioneers," " The Call of Eireann," and " The Watchword of Labour " shortly became favourite melodies during the many route-marches of the Army.

Many striking and original festivals were held in the beautiful grounds of Croydon Park. Features were introduced into these that were never seen before in Irish-Ireland Aeridheachteanna. The first event held was an astonishing and most embarrassing success. It had been splendidly advertised, and the crowds attending were so enormous that most of the items on the programme had to be abandoned, and it was only by the kind and herculean efforts of Messrs. Burke and Harty, of the Gaelic Athletic Association, that the committee succeeded in running the five miles Marathon race, which event provoked the wildest enthusiasm of the onlookers. It was amusing and humanly tragic to watch the despairing efforts of the stewards to evolve order out of hopeless and irremediable chaos. Everybody was looking for everybody else; no systematic communication could be kept up between the different workers, for between each was always a dense, surging and impassable crowd. Bands played, artistes sang, and children danced desperately at the same moment. Jin Larkin hurried frantically about from place to place, threatening the stewards that if they did not do something he would send the people home; and the gallant Countess Markievicz tried frequently to be in ten places at the one time. By superhuman efforts the " Citizen Army's Attack on a Cowboy Stockade " was carried through, and this spectacular event, with the advancing army taking cover and firing as they advanced, the little stockade fringed by swaying trees, from which came sharp and savage fusilades, the closing in on the defenders, and their ultimate capture from the midst of the blazing stockade was a scene that was rapturously acclaimed, and well repaid the disordered tedium of the early evening; and when the Park was emptied of its huge assembly, tired stewards crept towards Croydon Park House, and in the deepening shadows began to count the gains of the day, ever and anon ejaculating, "Thanks be with God that it's all over!"

During the summer Croydon Park was used by groups of the workers as a night camp, and this practice gave to the army life a realistic emotion that was pleasurable to many natures. The rank and file slept in the huge marquee, beside which were pitched two small tents, one for the Commandant, Jim Larkin, and the other for the use of the Council officers that elected to spend the week-end in that way.

Each member was charged a shilling, and for this on Sunday morning he received at 6 a.m. a substantial bowl of milk and porridge, to be followed at eight by a satisfying breakfast of bacon, eggs, bread, butter and tea.

Though situated well within the boundaries of the city, Croydon Park was singularly pastoral and peaceful. Here indeed one could rest at ease "far from the madding crowd's ignoble strife," and its restful influence had a powerful potency for good in bringing the workers closer to the warm, beautiful, pulsing heart of Nature.

It was beautiful to sit at the door of one of the tents on a camp stool, and dreamily survey the surrounding scene: The fading May-blossoms, the petals of which strewed the grass like confetti on the shimmering wedding garments of Summer. The tarnished gold of a laburnum tree, that gleamed redly in the rays of the declining sun. The tall chestnut trees whose waxy blooms, like fat and fairy caudles, now " 'gan to pale their diminished fires," and to view, here and there, beneath the sheltering arms of the lusty hedge, the ruby saucer-like blooms of the scarlet poppies as yet untouched by the childish vandals of the Irish Transport Union.

The surrounding trees were swaying clumps of melody which sprang from the swelling throats of numerous finches and linnets, and, sometimes, one was forced to ask the question, was all the strife with which man's life was coloured a shining light or a gloomy shade?

At times·the stillness would be so strange that one would wonder if it were not death to again associate with man's noisy, selfish effort to explain and manifest human existence.

Ah, this book of Nature is the best Bible from which to learn charity towards all men and love towards all things.

" Now fades the glimmering landscape on the sight,
      And all the air a solemn stillness holds,
Save where the beetle wheels his drowning flight,
      And drowsy tinklings lull the distant folds."

Here, with one's head in the bosom of Nature, to what a small compass shrinks even the Constitution of the Irish Citizen Army! How horrible is a glistening, oily rifle to one of the tiny daisies, that cowers in a rosy sleep at my very feet, happy in itself, and giving to the world to which it has been born the fullest beauty and fragrance that its simple nature has to give.

And then rings out with exasperating shrillness, the bugle-call declaring that it is time to retire, and as discipline is very strict in the night-camp, and the officer of the watch will shortly go his rounds to see that all is well, we leave the presence of the still redly-tinted sky, and withdraw to our tent, stretch ourselves upon the stretcher-bed, pull the blankets over our bodies, and try to go to sleep—to sleep—perchance to dream, and to wait till the loud notes of the Reveille wake us up at six o'clock on Sunday morning to make ready for the morning church-parade.

CHAPTER VII

SOME GENERAL EVENTS

" For in and out, above, about, below,
'Tis nothing but a magic shadow's show,
Play'd in a box, whose candle is the sun,
Around which we phantom figures come and go!"
—OMAR KHÀYYAM.

FOR some time Captain White had expressed dissatisfaction with the members attending the various parades, and finally signified his intention of resigning if conditions were not improved. But the difficulties surrounding the assemblies of the Citizen Army were so great, owing to the singular hours of the men's employment, that no appreciable improvement could be maintained, and in 1914 Captain White definitely severed his connection with the Citizen Army, and Jim Larkin was elected to the vacant position.

It is only fair to say that a quiet reflection of past events convinces the writer that Captain White did not obtain the ready and affectionate co-operation his nature craved for.

His efforts to understand the mysterious natures of working-men were earnest and constant, and were never fully appreciated by those amongst whom he spent his time and a good deal of his money.

But we feel sure that he will never be forgotten by those who knew him and worked by his side for many months.

He was a gentleman according, as Mitchel says, " to the British State and Constitution," but he was also a gentleman according to the kindly and benevolent law of Nature, and those who sat with him on the Council, and differed from him most, now wish to express their sincere affection for one who honestly and unselfishly endeavoured to use his gifts, natural and acquired, to lift the workers to a higher plane of usefulness and comfort.

Event succeeded event in the progress of the Citizen Army. The banner, the idea of which was given by a sympathiser, and executed by Mr. McGahey, was generally admired, and its symbolic design of the Plough and the Stars was indeed strikingly original. The tallest man in the army was selected as banner-bearer, and he was always proud of his work, though the carrying of the flag, which was of large dimensions, was no easy task, particularly upon a breezy day.

A rifle-range was erected in Croydon Park, and in the evening Volunteers and members of the Citizen Army vied with each other in trying to demonstrate the peculiar skill of their several organisations. The summer evenings in Croydon Park were peaceful no longer, and as the Park was approached, the cannonade of the terrible Howth guns smote the ear, and formed the impression that the place was the practice ground of batteries of heavy artillery.

In 1914 an elaborate plan had been sketched by Jim Larkin for the organisation of all Ireland, and he spent some weeks designing a suitable travelling caravan, which was to consist of a living room and two small bedrooms, in which he and a few chosen followers were to tour the country, and to form companies of the Army in every hamlet and village in Ireland. It was a pity that circumstances prevented this scheme from being definitely carried out, for it would have given to the Irish Labour

Movement a strength and a cohesion which was sadly needed, and the results would have been tremendously more effective than even those attained by his celebrated " Fiery Cross " campaign throughout England.

For many years to come the Irish people will follow leaders rather than principles, and in Larkin Labour had a leader for whom the Irish rural workers were waiting.

But the proposed scheme never materialised, and the Labour Movement and the Citizen Army were left to flourish as best they could in the industrial districts and the rural parts of county Dublin.

The divided difference in Ideal still flowed freely between the Volunteers and the Citizen Army, though on many occasions fraternal minglings testified of the deeper mutual understanding that existed between the two organisations. The incidents that took place during the celebrated episode of the Howth gun-running had engendered a fellow-feeling between the rank and file of both movements, which was very near akin to comradeship.

At the funeral of the victims that took place in Dublin, subsequent to the unfortunate shooting in Bachelor's Walk, the guards of honour around the funeral corteges were composed of alternate units of members of the Citizen Army and Volunteers.

CHAPTER VIII

MARKING TIME

" In such times as these it is not meet that every nice offence should bear its comment."

—JULIUS CÆSAR.

By their action in surrendering to the demand of the Parliamentary Party for the inclusion of a large number of nominees upon their Provisional Éxecutive, the Volunteers made the cleavage of principle between themselves and the Citizen Army deeper than ever. By this inexplicable action the last link of tacit sympathy and union was broken. Whatever hope Labour had of the evolution of a progressive policy from the Volunteer movement was now utterly abandoned, and the Citizen Army was forced in defence of the aims of militant Labour to become more antagonistic in thought and action towards the Volunteers than ever before.

Trenchant articles denouncing the compact appeared in the Labour Press from the pen of Jim Larkin, and biting cartoons illustrative of the situation were drawn and published by " E. K." pictorially ridiculing the union of opposite forces. All hope of an eventual junction between the Citizen Army and the Volunteers was shattered, and, day by day, it became increasingly evident that in aim and objects the two forces were marching towards opposite poles. The National Volunteers, through the action of their Executive, had definitely joined hands with Labour's bitterest enemies, and Labour's only attitude could be one of bitter suspicion and militant opposition towards the results that were expected from the new amalgamation.

But the new situation which had so unexpectedly been created caused a division in the Counoil of the Irish Citizen Army itself.

A special meeting of the Council was summoned by the Secretary to discuss the possibility of members of the Council being allowed to continue an active and sympathetic connection with the Volunteer Movement. This thrust was aimed purposely at the Countess Markievicz, whom the Secretary knew to be actively sympathetic with the Volunteers, and to hold an official position on the Committee of one of the branches of Cumann na mBan, the women's auxiliary movement, to advance the cause of the Volunteers. The Council assembled, and there were present : Countess Markievicz, Richard Brannigan, S. Rogan, J. Fitzpatrick, P. O'Brien, J. O'Leary, T. Blair, T. Healy, P. J. Fox, J. McGowan, H. Broderick, T. Foran, M. Mullen, Sean Shelly, who presided, and the Secretary, S. O Cathasaigh.

The following was the motion moved by the Honorary Secretary :

" Seeing that Madame Markievicz was, through Cumann na mBan, attached to the Volunteers, and on intimate terms with many of the Volunteer leaders, and as the Volunteers' Association was, in its methods and aims, inimical to the first interests of Labour, it could not be expected that Madame could retain the confidence of the Council; and that she be now asked to sever her connection with either the Volunteers or the Irish Citizen Army."

The Secretary briefly pointed out the reasons he had for bringing forward the resolution, and remarked that he felt it was the most honest course to pursue, to state frankly to the Council and to Madame Markievicz the thoughts that filled his mind respecting her connection with an association with which the Irish Citizen Army differed so widely.

The resolution was vigorously opposed by Messrs. Fox, Foran, Brannigan, Broderick and Rogan, and, after a warm discussion, a vote of confidence in the Countess was proposed by H. Broderick, seconded by P. J. Fox, and carried by seven votes to six.

It was then moved that the Secretary be called upon to tender an apology to Countess Markievicz, and to this the meeting apparently agreed.

The Secretary said he could not apologise for saying what he believed to be the truth, and wrote out his resignation, which was accepted at a Council meeting held a few days following.

The Commandant, Jim Larkin, was anxious to avoid all appearances of disunion, and he called a general meeting of members to consider the whole question, which meeting was held in the Concert Room, Liberty Hall, which was filled with the members of the Army.

Jim explained the whole circumstances of the attack made upon the Countess, and sincerely deprecated it. He appealed to the Secretary to withdraw anything he had said, and allow everything in the army to proceed smoothly without friction or unnecessary contention.

The Secretary briefly said he was sorry he could not do as Jim suggested, and that his decision was definite and final.

After some warm remonstrance on the part of the Commandant towards those whom he said evidently lacked the broadmindedness one would expect from them, the meeting harmoniously concluded by all of those present, excepting two members, taking the pledge to only serve and obey in a military capacity the officers of an Irish Republic.

CHAPTER IX

SOME INCIDENTS, AND LARKIN'S DEPARTURE

" Slan as ceud on dtaoibh seo uaim,
   Cois Maige na gcaor, na gcraobh, na gcruach,
   Na staid, na seud, na saor, na sluagh,
   Na ndan, na ndreacha, na dtreun gan gruaim !"
                                        —MAGRATH.

EVENTS began to follow each other in rapid succession.
The Citizen Army was watching anxiously the trend of
revolutionary thought in the ranks of the Volunteers, and
were delighted when the facts became known that the
Provisional Committee were returning to first principles,
and had overthrown their original acceptance of nomina-
tion to the Committee, and had determined to submit the
election of the governing Executive to a democratically-
elected Convention, which it was proposed to hold in the
near future.

The Irish Citizen Army had undergone a great change
in the personnel of its Army Council, which now had a
new Secretary, J. Connolly, and afterwards Sean Shelly,
Michael Mallon, W. Halpin and M. Nolan were included
on the Executive, and all the members were mentally
disturbed by the rumours that were gathering fast about
the contemplated departure of their Commandant, Jim
Larkin, for America.

On Saturday, October the 10th, a stop press edition of
The Worker announced that the Parnell anniversary
would be observed by the Volunteers the following day,

and a procession would take place to Glasnevin, after which a public meeting would be held in Parnell Square.

Burning interest was manifested by the workers and the Citizen Army in this event, for it became generally known that Jim Larkin had received an invitation to speak at the meeting. This was something unprecedented in the history of the National and Labour Movement in Ireland. That the leaders of the National Movement should not only allow, but actually invite, the Labour Leader to participate in a meeting organised by them opened up a possibility of definite unity and progress undreamt of a few short months before. The Citizen Army jubilantly hailed this overture as a certain indication of a desire on the part of the Volunteers to recognise the aims and aspirations of the Irish working class.

There is still a good deal of mystery surrounding this invitation. Whence it came no one seemed to know. It was afterwards generally believed that Jim, through perhaps a natural misunderstanding, took a general invitation to Labour to participate for a particular invitation to himself to speak at the meeting on behalf of the Citizen Army and the Labour Movement generally.

Some thought that the invitation was purposely issued by the more militant section of the Irish Volunteer Executive with a view of fixing an unbreakable bond on militant Nationalism and Labour.

That Jim Larkin received some kind of an invitation is certain, and that he mistook the full tenour of its meaning is very probable.

However, when the meeting was opened in Parnell Square, under the chairmanship of Mr. John MacNeill, it became clearly evident, when the Labour Leader approached the platform, that his presence was undesirable.

A most unhappy and embarrassing situation was immediately created, for an open and irremediable rupture between Labour and Nationalism was at once threatened. This unfortunate assurance was, happily, averted by the prompt and determined action of Tom Clarke and Sean MacDermott, who took measures to hold an independent meeting themselves, at which Jim Larkin and other Labour leaders spoke.

During the course of the meeting an exciting incident occurred which for a time threatened to have a tragic ending. A strong contingent of National Volunteers, returning from the march to Glasnevin, attempted to break through the crowd surrounding the speakers, and; by Jim Larkin's orders, the members of the Citizen Army deployed across the road and prepared to resist the attempt. These were shortly after joined by a strong force of Irish Volunteers under the command of Captains Monteith and Fahy, and for more than half an hour it seemed inevitable that a serious collision would take place between the united forces of the Volunteer and Citizen Army and the National Volunteers, who appeared for a time to be determined to force an issue.

Fortunately wiser counsels prevailed, and the National Volunteers faced right about and marched away in the opposite direction, followed by a cheer from the opposing party, which was instantly suppressed by the various officers, who deprecated strongly any indication of triumph at the discomfiture of brother Irishmen.

This day was memorable for the fact that it was the first time that the Irish Citizen Army and the Irish Volunteers had officially united in action and had unmistakably demonstrated the affinity of thought and ideal that existed between the two organisations.

A short time after these exciting incidents happened, the time came for Jim Larkin to say farewell to the Citizen Army and to Ireland, to undertake a tour in

America for the purpose, as he declared himself, of benefiting the Union of which he was Secretary, and to explain to American Labour the aims and aspirations of the Irish Proletariat.

In the *Irish Worker* of October the 24th, 1914, appeared Jim Larkin's farewell message to the members of the Citizen Army :—

." To my Comrades of the Irish Citizen Army :

" In my absence Jim Connolly will take command. Bear yourselves before all men according to your past.

" Remember your constitution and your oath—Ireland first, last, and all the time.   Sobriety, unquestioned obedience, and keenness for drill be your motto."

And then this fiery human comet passed from the orbit of Irish life, to be attracted back again by the power of its heat—when?   Ah! who can say?

CHAPTER X

JIM CONNOLLY ASSUMES THE LEADERSHIP

" My country claims me all, claims every passion ;
  Her liberty henceforth be all my thought !
  Though with a brother's life yet cheaply bought ;
  For her my own I'd willingly resign,
  And say, with transport, that the gain was mine."
                                        —MARTYN.

UNDER Jim Connolly's leadership an appreciable change
began to appear in the attitude of the Citizen Army
Council towards the Volunteers. The attitude of
passive sympathy began to be gradually replaced by an
attitude of active unity and co-operation. In their
break-away from the control of the Parliamentarian
Party the Volunteers had built a bridge over the stream
of thought that separated the two forces from each other,
and speculation became common as to whether the Volunteers would absorb the Citizen Army or that body's
influence would sway the councils of the Volunteers.
Jim Connolly had never associated himself with any of
the attacks made upon the Volunteers during their
earlier history—indeed, whenever he had previously
interested himself in the affairs of the Citizen Army,
which was seldom, his influence had been invariably
exerted to moderate the mutual hostility that smouldered,
and occasionally flamed, into passionate recriminations—
and, consequently, the relations between him and the

militant members of the Volunteer Council soon became cordial. It is difficult to understand the almost revolutionary change that was manifesting itself in Connolly's nature. The Labour movement seemed to be regarded by him as a decrescent force, while the essence of Nationalism began to assume the finest elements of his nature. His articles that now appeared in the *Workers' Republic* with consistent regularity, the speeches that he delivered at various demonstrations and assemblies, all proclaimed that Jim Connolly had stepped from the narrow byway of Irish Socialism on to the broad and crowded highway of Irish Nationalism. The vision of the suffering world's humanity was shadowed by the nearer oppression of his own people, and in a few brief months pressed into a hidden corner of his soul the accumulated thoughts of a lifetime and opened his broad heart to ideas that altered the entire trend of his being. The high creed of Irish Nationalism became his daily rosary, while the higher creed of international humanity that had so long bubbled from his eloquent lips was silent for ever, and Irish Labour lost a Leader.

A well-known author has declared that Connolly was the first martyr for Irish Socialism; but Connolly was no more an Irish Socialist martyr than Robert Emmett, P. H. Pearse, or Theobald Wolfe Tone.

But as this little work is intended to be historical rather than critical, we must take up again the simple and concise narration of the facts as they occurred.

The Constitution of the Irish Volunteers was radically altered on Sunday, October 25th, 1914, at the first Convention held by that organisation in the Abbey Theatre, Dublin. The Convention was called after the original Provisional Executive had definitely repudiated the government of the nominees which Mr. J. E. Redmond had selected to ensure that the Irish Volunteer movement would be always subsidiary to the Constitutional agitation carried on by the Parliamentary Party in favour of self-government for Ireland. The Volunteer movement had been riven in sunder and two distinct branches now called upon the people of Ireland for support and allegiance : the National Volunteers under the patronage of the Parliamentarians, and the Irish Volunteers under the government of the original Executive Committee.

Force of circumstances compelled the Irish Volunteers and the Citizen Army to link forces together on many occasions. Their sympathies at least became identical in hostility to everything connected with the Parliamentarian Party. The members of the two movements began to fraternise together, and on the day of the Convention the members of the Citizen Army helped to line the roads leading to the Abbey Theatre, in which the Volunteer Convention was held, and gave many indications of their feeling of exultation at the formation of a Volunteer Association which had been largely purged of what they considered to be reactionary elements, and which had formulated a Constitution which evoked their sympathies and commanded their support. To all that carefully reflected upon passing events it was apparent that the Citizen Army was really becoming the militant Left Wing of the Irish Volunteers.

Referring to the Convention, the *Irish Worker,* October 31st, 1914, said :—" We congratulate the Volunteers on the success they have achieved. It is a significant sign, and should give Irishmen here at home reason to pause to see Volunteer delegates from London, Glasgow and Liverpool taking part in the proceedings and standing side by side with the true men in the movement. They have not forgotten the hellish system which forced them to seek a living in the land of the stranger."

At a great Emmett Anniversary held on Sunday,

October the 25th, organised by the Irish Volunteers, the Irish Citizen Army attended in full strength, and the following notice in the *Irish Worker* indicated the desire of the Volunteers to enlist on their side the power and influence of Labour :—

IRISH VOLUNTEERS' FIRST ANNUAL CONVENTION,

SUNDAY, OCTOBER 25th.

GREAT DEMONSTRATION AND TORCHLIGHT PROCESSION

Around places in this city sacred to the memory of the United Irishmen and other patriots who died for Ireland. To be concluded by a

MEETING IN STEPHEN'S GREEN,

at which a declaration of the policy adopted by this Convention will be made.

All Nationalist and Labour Bodies and Bands are invited to co-operate.

Procession will assemble in Beresford Place at 6.30 prompt.

Mr. EOIN MACNEILL will speak.

It became quite obvious now to all that the Irish Volunteers and the Citizen Army were essentially one in ideal, and would eventually be one in action. Things were hurrying towards a bloody climax, but as yet the cloud in the sky was no larger than a man's hand, and no one realized that in a few weeks it would have enveloped the whole of the City of Dublin in smoke and blood and fire.

The drilling of the Volunteers and the Citizen Army

daily became more pointed and practical; and in the manœuvres practised by both organisations, it became apparent that everything possible was being done to prepare their members to make the most of their limited numbers and circumscribed powers.

A further indication of the singular change in Jim Connolly's ideas, and of his determined attachment to the principles enunciated by Sinn Fein and the Irish Volunteers, which were, in many instances, directly contrary to his life-long teaching of Socialism, was the fixing on the frontage of Liberty Hall a scroll on which was written the inscription : " We serve neither King nor Kaiser—but Ireland." His speeches and his writings had long indicated his new trend of thought, and his actions now proclaimed trumpet-tongued that the appeal of Caitlin Ni hUllachain—" If anyone would give me help, he must give me himself, he must give me all "—was in his ears a louder cry than the appeal of the Internationale, which years of contemplative thought had almost written in letters of fire upon his broad and noble soul.

Liberty Hall was now no longer the Headquarters of the Irish Labour movement, but the centre of Irish National disaffection. Activities redoubled ; preparations went forward with feverish haste, and the night was made joint labourer with the day. Route marches were organised, and carried out at every conceivable hour with order, and disciplined enthusiasm, and no member of the Citizen Army knew when he retired to bed how long he might be allowed to repose there, for frequent summonses were issued to members to join their units at an hour's notice to go they knew not where, and do they knew not what.

One day everyone entering Liberty Hall was startled to read on the notice-board that that night the Irish Citizen Army was to make an attack upon Dublin Castle, and many a conjecture was framed as to the seriousness of the purpose indicated on the notice-board. At midnight out marched the Citizen Army under their leaders, through a heavy fog that enveloped the city, the mist-shaded electric street lamps blinking at this body of armed men marching by, like watchful eyes eagerly endeavouring to discover the reason of this unusual and singular sight in the streets of Dublin at such an hour.

But it was only a test, and these practices continued making the members used to sudden calls, and generally preparing them for the heavy struggle that was soon to break the gentle and happy sleepiness of Dublin City.

A definite union had now been formed between the Irish Citizen Army and the Irish Volunteers, and on the Sunday before Easter Day, 1916, an outward and visible sign of the inward union was given by the dramatic hoisting of the Irish Tricolour, of Orange, Green and White, over the most conspicuous part of Liberty Hall.

On the evening of the ceremonial, thousands thronged the square in front of the Hall, and as the ball of bunting flew up the flagstaff, shook itself free on the breeze, and contrasted its lines of Green, White and Orange with a dull grey sky, there was a thunderclap of cheering which proclaimed unmistakably that the union of Labour and Militant Nationalism was a popular one, though many in the assembled crowd merely came to feast their souls on a novel pageant, which event is always a sweet luxury to the uneducated Irish nature.

Labour had laid its precious gift of Independence on the altar of Irish Nationalism, and this display was a sign to the governing classes to at least consider the dumb wish of an aspiring people.

It was followed by fire and bloodshed, and, as the great Englishman, Carlyle, says : " The governors who wait for these to instruct them are surely getting into the fatallest courses—proving themselves sons of Nox and

Chaos, for Insurrection is a mere announcement of the disease—visible now even to the Sons of Night . . . the falsehood of it alone will be conquered, will be abolished as it ought to be ; but the truth of it is part of Nature's own laws, co-operates with the world's eternal tendencies and cannot be conquered."

CHAPTER XI

THE RISING

" When the dark world seems all too desperate,
A hopeless, hideous struggle without cease,
When hope is gone what left but seek release
In one mad grapple with the thing you hate;
Flinging all counsel to the whirlwind, send
Defiant challenge to the world ; and so
Recklessly facing your triumphant foe,
Pray that some welcome bullet bring the end.

" Yours was this grim resolve that nerves the will
When faith and hope are fled beyond recall,
As it was theirs who died at Bunker Hill,
And those mad boys who held the Roman Wall ;
Your dreams, maybe, were madmen's dreams; but
still
You gave your lives for them—God rest you all !"
    —W. N. EWEN, " The Five Souls."

FROM the blue skies was falling a golden curtain of
shimmering sunshine, clothing buildings in its filmy
cloth of gold, and veiling their naked ugliness in beauty,
or adding a richer appearance to their classic grace and
strength.

It was a day on which to make merry, and crowded
streets proclaimed that the influences of the sun's
geniality was making melody in the hearts of man.

Many were climbing joyously on to the trams to seek
in Nature's bosom a place that would hide them for a
few hours " far from the madding crowd's ignoble
strife," while distinct gatherings of people stood by near
Nelson Pillar and found happy moments in the contemplation of the passing activities of human life.
Curious glances were flung at passing vehicles, burdened
with hopeful crews, flashing swiftly by on their way to
Fairyhouse Races, and the pulse of human anxiety was
scarcely felt besides the quick-beating pulse of human
enjoyment.

Now the holiday seekers were disregarded for an addi-
tional novelty; the cars for Fairyhouse went speeding
by unnoticed, and a semi-lazy but curious concentration
of attention was fixed on an approaching body of marching men.

Passengers on the tram cars leisurely approached the
sides and looked down on the armed force, and won-
dered vaguely at the sharp order to halt, as they came
in front of the General Post Office. " Those there,"
said someone, " dressed in the dark-green uniforms, with
the slouch hats, are the Citizen Army, and the others in
green-grey are Irish Volunteers."

The curiosity displayed in the proceedings gave place
now to bewildered astonishment as the ring of falling
glass echoed from the direction of the Post Office.
Astonishment was followed by stupefaction as faint echoes
of rifle shots penetrated from a distance to where the
people were gathered together, and all things were forgotten as the news spread from mouth to mouth that the
Volunteers and the Citizen Army were taking Dublin,
that a Provisional Government had been established and
an Irish Republic proclaimed.

At three o'clock p.m. on Easter Monday the

General Post Office was occupied by the united forces, and separate detachments of the Citizen Army were marching on Stephen's Green and on Dublin Castle.

The contingent that took possession of Stephen's Green was in command of Michael Mallon. Countess Markievicz was second in command, and detachments were hastily sent to hold the advanced positions of Harcourt Street Station and Ranelagh Bridge till the Green could be advantageously arranged for occupation by the main body of the Citizen Army. Owing to the fewness of the contingent that operated in this district, it was found to be impossible to take possession of the surrounding buildings, and, consequently, the position became untenable, and it was abandoned on Tuesday morning, the Citizen Army retreating under heavy machine-gun fire to the College of Surgeons, which they immediately fortified as best they could, and where they were reinforced by a detachment of Volunteers from Jacob's biscuit factory.

The company which attacked the Castle was under the command of Shaun Connolly, who was fatally wounded in the *melee*. For hours a bitter struggle raged in the Castle Yard, in Henry and James', Parliament Street, and in the *Mail* offices, during which this little band, contending against hopeless odds, suffered severely, and were finally forced to gradually withdraw to stronger positions nearer the Headquarters of the Republican Army.

On Thursday morning the attack on the Republican Headquarters commenced. Field Artillery had cleared away many of the intervening buildings, and incendiary bombs were dropped in regular order on the roof of the Post Office. Blazing buildings surrounded them on every side. Most of their faces were blood-stained; the skin was chipped from their cheeks by flying fragments of stone and mortar, and, occasionally, the bright flame of the burning Post Office would be stabbed by the dark shadow of a falling man. Connolly, who had been wounded twice, was carried, by his orders, from the room that was being used as an hospital to superintend the withdrawal from the front defences, and it became clear that if the little band was not to be buried in the tottering masses of timber and stone, an immediate retreat was inevitable.

On Friday night, between 8.30 and 9.30, the retreat began from the side entrance of the Post Office, into Moore Lane, where a party held a cottage facing Glass Marble Alley, up which, from behind a barricade, a contingent of soldiers were firing rapidly at the passing Volunteers and Citizen Army.

A plan had been determined upon which was to break through the houses in Moore Street towards Parnell Street, in which there was a strong force of soldiers. These were to be attacked and driven back by a picked company of Volunteers, and the main body was then to seize the premises of Williams and Woods, link up with the detachments fighting in North King Street, and beat a fighting retreat towards the north in order to make an effort to arouse the companies of Volunteers and sympathisers who, it was thought, only waited a definite opportunity to throw in their lot with the Irish Republicans.

It was discovered that, owing to the superiority of the Royal troops, this attack, arranged to take place at dawn, could not possibly succeed, and it was accordingly postponed till the dusk of the evening, so that the element of surprise might, conceivably, make up for the numerical weakness of the Republican attacking force, and orders were given to the men to take such rest as might be possible under the circumstances that surrounded them.

A few hours after rumours were circulated that communications had been commenced with the General Commanding to ascertain the best possible conditions which would be given to the Republican forces should a surrender be decided upon, the rumour being shortly confirmed by an order that no shots should be fired pending the discussion that was then taking place between the leaders of the opposing armies.

At 8.30 on Saturday night, April the 29th, the men were definitely told that surrender had been decided upon, and Sean MacDermott, his whole frame shaking with emotion, in the yard of a house in Moore Street, spoke to the silent gathering of dust-covered men, gloomily sharing the half-suppressed agony of their leader, and told them " that their Republican Army had surrendered, not because they were beaten, but because they wanted to save their women and children and their beloved city of Dublin. They would march out with their arms through Moore Street, Henry Street, to O'Connell Street, where they would lay down arms."

In the gathering shadows of a spring evening the small band of men, who had passed through such a terrible experience, marched in order of company column to the statue of Parnell, where, in the centre of O'Connell Street, they deposited their arms and accoutrements, which step was shortly augmented by the arms of the different contingents arriving from the various, parts of the city.

AFTERWORD.

" Iram indeed is gone with all its Rose,
   And Jamshyd's Seven-ring'd Cup where no one knows;
   But still the Vine her ancient Ruby yields,
   And still a Garden by the water blows."
                                    —OMAR KHAYYAM.

THE breath of Death which had swept over poor Dublin
carried with it the seeds of a new life, which, falling in
different parts of Ireland, began to appear as green blades
of new thought and new activities. The bonfires of Sinn
Fein began to blaze on every Irish hillside, and thousands
of the Irish people danced around the blaze of Sinn Fein,
as if they warmed themselves at the fire of life. Parliamentarianism was a sinking fire, and, now, not all the
united breath of a united party could ever again succeed
in blowing it into an inspiring flame. The new wine of
new thoughts and new activities was everywhere bursting
the old bottles, but though the new wine has a Sinn Fein
label it certainly has not an absolutely Sinn Fein flavour,
for Labour has tinged it with a brighter colour and
strengthened it with a stimulating cordial.

In this new wine a lowly life, like a pearl, had been
dissolved; a life untarnished by worldly ambition, or
selfish perception; a life of mourning struggle and valor-
ous effort sacrificed humbly and fearlessly for the general
good; sacrificed under circumstances that stripped the
offering of all the impressive draperies of martyrdom.
Unwept, except by a few, unhonoured and unsung—for

no National Society or Club has gratefully deigned to be called by his name—yet the ideas of Sheehy-Skeffington, like the tiny mustard seed to-day, will possibly grow into a tree that will afford shade and rest to many souls overheated with the stress and toil of barren politics. He was the living antithesis of the Easter Insurrection : a spirit of peace enveloped in the flame and rage and hatred of the contending elements, absolutely free from all its terrifying madness ; and yet he was the purified soul of revolt against not only one nation's injustice to another, but he was also the soul of revolt against man's inhumanity to man. And in this blazing pyre of national differences his beautiful nature, as far as this world is concerned, was consumed, leaving behind a hallowed and inspiring memory of the perfect love that casteth out fear, against which there can be no law.

In Sheehy-Skeffington, and not in Connolly, fell the first martyr to Irish Socialism, for he linked Ireland not only with the little nations struggling for self-expression, but with the world's Humanity struggling for a higher life.

He indeed was the ripest ear of corn that fell in Easter Week, and as it is true that when an ear of corn falls into the ground and dies it bringeth forth much fruit, so will the sown body of Sheehy-Skeffington bring forth, ultimately, in the hearts of his beloved people, the rich crop of goodly thoughts which shall strengthen us all in our onward march towards the fuller development of our National and Social Life.

.   .   .   .   .   .

One of the most gratifying and encouraging indications of the broader and kindlier vision of human nature was the earnest sympathy expressed towards the Irish people by many of the leaders of thought among the English people, subsequent to the sad events of Easter Week. Nowhere in England, among the working classes, was manifested that insensate outburst of rage and malice that invariably characterised the attitude of England's workers towards Irish people during previous Irish declarations of revolt towards the English domination. It has certainly demonstrated that even the English workers have been potently influenced by the change of thought that has enwrapped man in a new and better social environment. Sympathy and kindly feeling towards Ireland were manfully expressed in many places in England during this period of sorrow and sacrifice, which ought to convince even the most bigoted of Sinn Feiners of the truth testified to by Boyle O'Reilly and John Mitchel in the fundamental unity of man.

George Lansbury, speaking at a great meeting held in Albert Hall, to commemorate the Russian Revolution, said : " We English people have to clear our own doorstep. I stood here just about three years ago; almost where Williams is sitting sat James Connolly (cheers). He and his dead colleagues of a year ago were just too soon, that is all ; and, friends, we British people have got to clear that Irish question up, because until we do it, it is not for us to celebrate other people's triumphs over reaction.'' And in many English Labour papers the writings of Jim Connolly have been quoted, and his Labour songs published, so that these and many other indications conclusively prove that the mind of the English working class has undergone a revolutionary change, and that "the unbought section of the English Labour movement "—to quote from *Nationality*—is seriously anxious to stretch forth the hand of true comradeship towards their Irish fellow-workers.

We laugh, frequently, at the efforts of English Governments and English journalists to understand us, and our amusement is invariably justified ; but let us at least make an effort to acquaint ourselves with the new 'trend of thought passing like a pillar of illuminating fire over England's workers, that we may know them as they are, before we unjustly and foolishly relegate this all-powerful element in England's political and social life among the irreconcilable enemies of Inisfail.

.   .   .   .   .   .

While the ultimate destiny of Ireland will be in the hands of Labour, it would be foolish to deny that the present is practically in the hands of the Sinn Fein Organisation. Its activities are spreading over the land, and Labour comes-halting very much behind. This is explained by two reasons : Sinn Fein is not yet democratic, though Irish ; while Labour, though fundamentally democratic, is far from being National. As Parliamentarianism was a poor copy of English Liberalism, so is Irish Labour a poorer reflex of English Trades Unionism. Its boasted Irish characteristics are far from being apparent, and its pretended love for the Irish language is very superficial indeed. It has done nothing to ensure that Irish shall be the language of the future nation ; its propaganda literature is practically written from an English point of view, and the Irish Labour leaders are all painfully ignorant of their country's history, language and literature. It is because of these self-evident facts that Sinn Fein possesses a tremendous advantage over the Labour movement. Persecution has deepened our sympathies with our Irish origin, and the Irish Labour leaders, sooner or later, will be forced to realise that they must become Irish if they expect to win the confidence and support of the Irish working-class. Sinn Fein, too, will have to cope with the greatest of all difficulties—success. Here now, like tares and wheat, the good and evil will grow up together. It will roughly be composed of two classes of thought : those who love themselves so well that they have none left for Ireland, and those who love Ireland so well that they have none left for themselves. The first love is selfish ; the second foolish.

It is from these elements that Labour must build the future state ; democratising the national movement and Irishising itself. Labour will probably have to fight Sinn Fein—indeed the challenge seems to have been thrown down already—but the Labour leaders must become wiser and more broadminded than they at present seem to be ; they must remove the beam from their own eye that they may clearly see to remove the mote from the eye of Sinn Fein, and then they will find in that organisation elements that will readily yield to its penetrating forces ; then the leaders of Labour in Ireland will be able to glean grapes from a tree that hitherto brought forth only wild grapes, because Labour, through the Citizen Army, has broken down the first trenches of national prejudice, and has left a deep impression on the bloody seal of Irish Republicanism.

APPENDIX

MANIFESTO SENT TO IRISH TRADES BODIES.

IRISH CITIZEN ARMY HEADQUARTERS,
LIBERTY HALL, DUBLIN.

The Secretary........................Trades Union.

A Chara,—In view of the present situation it has been decided to reorganise and develop the scope of the Irish Citizen Army. No one knows what a day may bring forth. We have the Ulster Volunteers preparing for eventualities in the North, and the National Volunteers actively organising themselves in various parts of Ireland, while all the time the Labour Hercules leans foolishly and lazily on his club.

Would it not be a shame if the forces of Labour alone were content to believe all things, suffer all things, endure all things; to starve rather than take, to be stricken and not to strike back?

Believing that Labour will shake itself to action, we have formed a Provisional Council to develop the power and influence of the Citizen Army in Labour circles, and we hope their efforts will receive the co-operation of your Trades Union. We propose to hold a meeting in your........................... shortly, and, in the meantime, we appeal to you to use your efforts to prevent the members of your Union from joining any organisation, however attractive its name or principles may seem, till we have the opportunity of fully explaining to them the principles, objects and aims of the Irish Citizen Army.

We enclose copies of Constitution, posters and hand-bills, and hope that these will show that the Irish Citizen Army is the only suitable organisation for the workers of Ireland.

Fraternally yours,
President, CAPTAIN WHITE, D.S.O.,
Hon. Secretary, SEAN O CATHASAIGH,
Irish Citizen Army.

FIRST HANDBILL ISSUED BY IRISH CITIZEN ARMY.

WHY IRISH WORKERS SHOULD NOT JOIN THE NATIONAL VOLUNTEERS!

1. Because many members of the Executive are hostile to the workers.
2. Because it is controlled by the forces that have always opposed Labour.
3. Because many of its officials have locked out their workers for asserting their right to join the Trades Union of their choice.
4. Because they refuse to definitely declare that they stand for the Democratic principles of Wolfe Tone and John Mitchel.
5. Because they welcome into their organisation creatures that are proved renegades to their own class.

REASONS WHY THE WORKERS SHOULD JOIN THE IRISH CITIZEN ARMY.

1. Because it is controlled by Leaders of your own class.

2. Because it stands for Labour and the principles of Wolfe Tone, John Mitchel and Fintan Lalor.

3. Because it has the sympathy and support of the Dublin Trades Council.

4. Because it refuses to allow in its ranks those who have proved untrue to Labour.

WORKERS, don't be misled; trust only those ye know and have suffered for your class.

JOIN THE CITIZEN ARMY NOW!

COPY OF MEMBERSHIP CARD.

FRONT PAGE.

THE IRISH CITIZEN ARMY MEMBERSHIP CARD, 1913.

President:
CAPTAIN WHITE, D.S.O.

Hon. Secretary:
SEAN O CATHASAIGH.

Hon. Treasurers:
COUNTESS MARKIEVICZ.
RICHARD BRANNIGAN.

Army Headquarters:
LIBERTY HALL, DUBLIN.

Go gCuiridh Dia an Rath Orainn.

Back Page.

" The Land and Sea and Air of Ireland for the People of Ireland. That is the gospel the heavens and earth are proclaiming; and that is the gospel every Irish heart is secretly burning to embrace."—*John Mitchel.*

THE CONSTITUTION OF THE IRISH CITIZEN ARMY.

1.—That the first and last principle of the Irish Citizen Army is the avowal that the ownership of Ireland, moral and material, is vested of right in the people of Ireland.

2.—That its principal objects shall be :—

a. To arm and train all Irishmen capable of bearing arms to enforce and defend its first principle.

b. To sink all differences of birth, privilege and creed under the common name of the Irish People.

3.—That the Citizen Army shall stand for the absolute unity of Irish Nationhood and recognition of the rights and liberties of the world's Democracies.

4.—That the Citizen Army shall be open to all who are prepared to accept the principles of equal rights and opportunities for the People of Ireland and to work in harmony with organised Labour towards that end.

5.—Every enrolled member must be, if possible, a member of a Trades Union recognised by the Irish Trades Union Congress.

GOD SAVE THE PEOPLE.

COPY OF FIRST POSTER ISSUED BY CITIZEN ARMY COUNCIL, 1914.

" Train your hands and your sons' hands, gentlemen of the earth, for you and they will have to use them."— FINTAN LALOR.

TO THE PEOPLE OF IRELAND.

This is the Time for Action. All political organisations are preparing for the future. Shall labour remain apathetic? Remember, workers, that

THE PRICE OF LiBERTY IS ETERNAL VIGILANCE.

Put the advice of Labour in practice by joining now

THE IRISH CITIZEN ARMY,

which stands for the Cause of Labour and erects its Constitution on the principles of

WOLFE TONE AND JOHN MITCHEL.

Enlist at once and help us to create

THE IRISH CO-OPERATIVE COMMONWEALTH.

GOD SAVE THE PEOPLE.

All particulars from
THE HONORARY SECRETARY,
Irish Citizen Army,
Liberty Hall,
Dublin.